WHAT IS The Day of Judgement?

This book belongs to:

____

24 23 22 21 1 2 3 4

Published by Tughra Books
335 Clifton Ave.
Clifton, NJ, 07011, USA
www.tughrabooks.com

ISBN: 979-8-89729-508-1

Mini Muslims Series ISBN 9781597849692

WHAT IS The Day of Judgement?

This life is a test to see

if we will do ..

good or bad

After we pass away

Allah will bring us all

back to life

Then Allah will start the day of judgement.

This is when you will see everything

you have done and Allah will judge you.

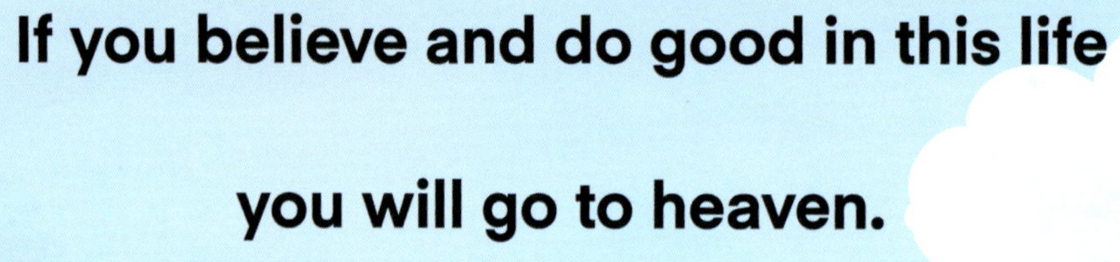

If you believe and do good in this life

you will go to heaven.

Heaven is called Jennah!

Let's all do our best

so we can be in Jennah

together inshallah!